Miss Forbes

First Day of School

Written By:
Rigelle Forbes

Illustrated By:
Katie African

It was the last Monday in August, the first day of school. Parents, grandparents and bus drivers were busy taking students to school. Anxiety filled the air as this would be the beginning of friendships that possibly could last a lifetime as the little ones would be meeting their teachers and new friends for the very first time.

The classroom was nicely arranged and vibrant colors displayed throughout the room; books and materials were neatly stacked to one corner of the room.

04

Miss Forbes stood patiently near her door to greet and welcome her special gifts. One by one the students entered the classroom filled with excitement and curiosity. Soon all students were seated and ready to begin their day.

At 8'oclock, the school bell rang. Miss Forbes quietly closed the door and stood before her eager class. Suddenly, something strange happened. All she could see was a great disaster! Gum bubbles popping, snack bags opening, students fighting, broken crayons on the floor, paper planes flying, students shouting and even chairs being turned upside down.

08

"Quiet! Quiet!" Miss Forbes yelled. "The next voice I hear, you will be going to the time out corner!" The entire class went silent as everyone was frightened.

"Where do you think you are?" asked Miss Forbes. "This is a classroom, certainly not an amusement park!" She said. "In five minutes my classroom must be fixed!" Miss Forbes strongly demanded. She set the white timer on her desk. The ticking sound was very loud. She noticed the sweat dripping from her students' faces as they were nervous and afraid. The students hurriedly worked as a team to clean up their mess. Miss Forbes watched with a keen eye. She insisted that the job be done right.

She looked at her timer and shouted in a cheering voice "4-3-2-1." The timer went off with a loud noise. All the students quickly rushed to their assigned seats. Miss Forbes walked quietly around the room with her pen and pad checking each team. She was so astonished to see how well her 2nd graders cleaned up the messy classroom. Zachary whispered," I never want to see Miss Forbes get so angry again." "Me too," whispered Jazmine.

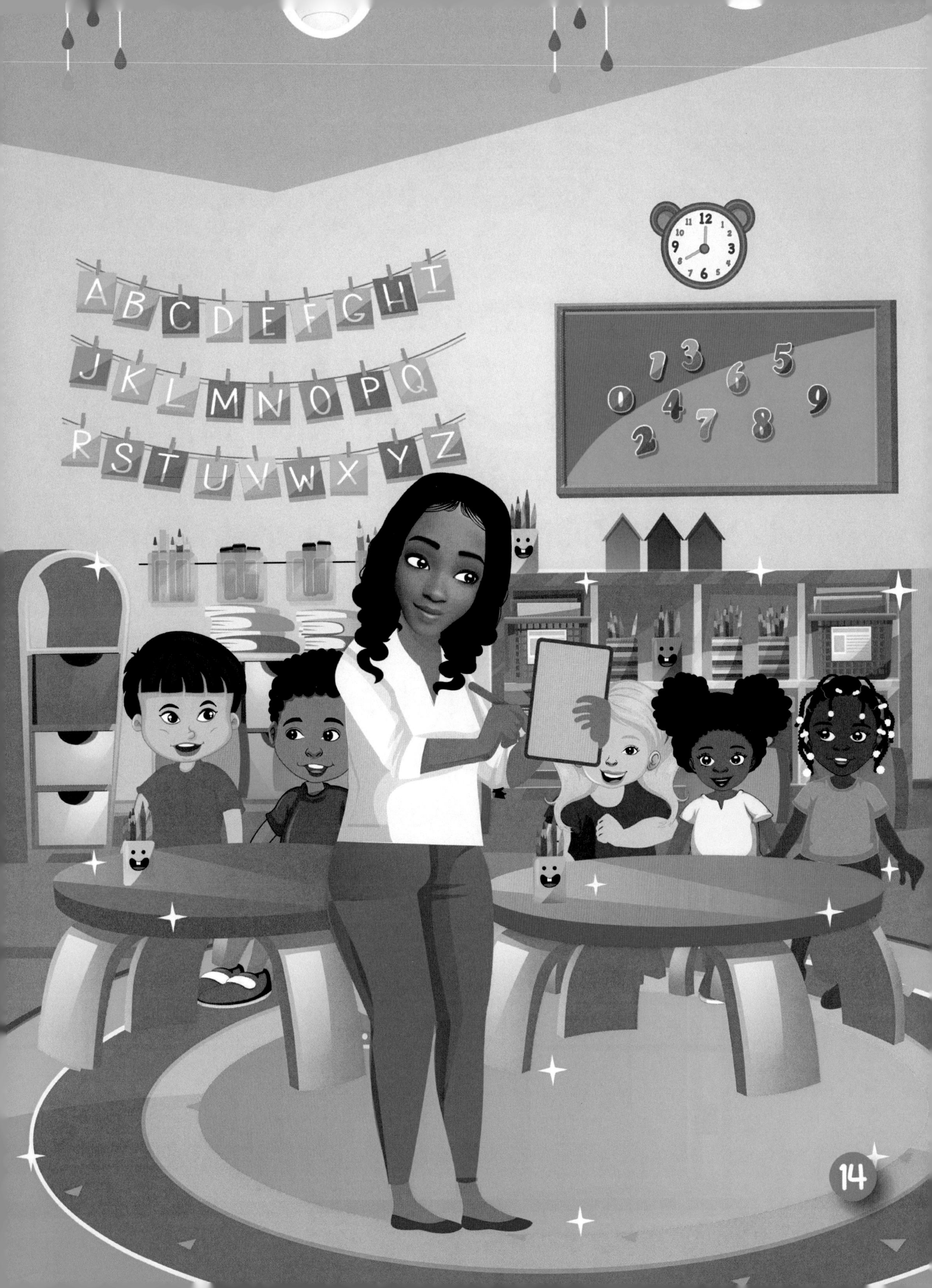
ABCDEFGHI
JKLMNOPQ
RSTUVWXYZ
1 3 5
0 4 6 9
2 7 8

Miss Forbes walked to the front of the room with a pleasant smile on her face, "Good morning class, I am Miss Forbes and I will be your homeroom teacher for this school year. It's my pleasure to have you in my class!
One thing you should know is that, I have rules and my rules you will follow!"
1..
2..
3... and the list went on.

After the students introduced themselves it was time for lunch. As the class bell rang, the students rushed out of their seats and ran to the line. "OH NO!" Miss Forbes said." Go back to your seats! That's definitely not how it's done. Another important rule is that we must do things in order. Table number one, you may line up."

The students walked quietly to the line. "Excellent!" Miss Forbes cheered. Each team lined up quietly. "Thank you!" Miss Forbes said. "Now while you're walking, catch a bubble with your mouth and hold your hands firmly by your sides". The students walked quietly to the cafeteria.

It was 12 o'clock, lunch was over. The students were nicely lined up as Miss Forbes inspected the lunch tables. "OH NO, GARBAGE, GARBAGE!" she exclaimed." We do not leave our garbage behind! We clean up!"

The students went back, cleaned up their tables and disposed of their garbage. With excitement she said, "Nice, now we can have recess."

At recess there was a big commotion, Monique and Cindy started to fight. "I was on the slide first!" shouted Monique. She pushed Cindy out of the way, Cindy pushed back and said "I was there first" and they continued to push. Miss Forbes ran over and shouted, Time out! She then reminded the students that we do not push each other. "The rest of you line up!" The students returned to the classroom. Miss Forbes discussed the school policy especially with regards to bullying and fighting.

"I know you will have differences, but there are many other ways to solve problems. We can learn to share and take turns. If trouble continues, then tell your teacher! I know you won't get it perfect at once but practice makes perfect".

Monique and Cindy understood what they did wrong. They shook hands and apologized to the class. It had been a very long day and the students were very tired. Miss Forbes looked at the clock near the window and noticed the dismissal bell would be ringing in about 25 minutes. She quickly passed out the important papers to be sent home.

Students quietly gathered their bookbags and followed the bus line up procedure. "Ready, Set, Go!" the class was on their way to the buses. Miss Forbes then raised her hand to high 5 the students as they were about to get on the bus.

Just then she heard the principal
called out "Miss Forbes,
Miss Forbes, do you have
a question?"
Miss Forbes looked puzzled,
as the other teachers chuckled.
"Were you daydreaming?"
The principal asked, and
handed her the class roster
for the new school term.
Remember now, school
starts tomorrow!

Made in the USA
Middletown, DE
02 September 2024

60309696R00018